The Teachings Of Atlantis

Secrets of the Cosmos

Michael Love

Sacred Light Publishing

Contents

Dedication

To my cherished wife and soulmate, Lara, this book is a testament to our shared voyage and the unbreakable bond we've nurtured. The depth of your love and the strength of your belief in me has been the compass guiding my path. With each page written, I've been reminded of the radiant beacon you are, illuminating the way for many. As we journey on, hand in hand, we continue to touch lives, creating ripples of positive change.

To the remarkable souls who've stood by me, offering encouragement and faith during this book's inception, your unwavering support has lit the fires of determination and creativity.

In deep appreciation,

Michael Love

Foreword

No other story has captured the fascination and curiosity of spiritual seekers throughout history as profoundly as the story of Atlantis. There is something very real about this story, an ancient echo reverberating deep within our souls, compelling us to explore its mysterious depths further. What distinguishes the account of Atlantis isn't just its enchanting allure; it's a direct recollection, an integral part of our very essence, rooted in a past life we once experienced during those revered days—an impactful memory eternally etched into our psyche.

In this narrative, you will discover the authentic history of the cosmos through the annals of the Emerald Founders and grasp how this history was distorted on Earth by the fallen races concealed from humanity. Follow the sequence of events that unfolded through the ages in the relentless struggle over human DNA, leading to the ultimate betrayal culminating in the fall of Atlantis.

'The Teachings Of Atlantis - Secrets of the Cosmos' invites you to explore the sacred sciences of ancient

Atlantis. Explore the astonishing advanced technologies wielded by this illustrious civilization and step into the enigmatic ancient mystery schools protected by the Melchizedeks and the Essenes, the Angelic Guardian Priests of sacred knowledge in Atlantis.

Experience the magnificence of Atlantis, where its mastery of crystal power stands as evidence of advanced understanding. In this narrative, discover a realm where mysticism and science harmoniously converge, where one could traverse through a Stargate and journey to another star system. Atlantis was a magical yet tangible world where divine beings walked among humanity on Earth.

As a new era of light dawns, 'The Teachings Of Atlantis - Secrets of the Cosmos' serves as an illuminating guidepost, reigniting the flames of ancestral memory and preparing humanity for their profound evolution of consciousness.

Chapter 1: **Atlantis Emerges**
The Emerald Library

"Cosmic wisdom is not written in the pages of books, but inside the human being, waiting for the curious heart to decode its timeless knowledge."

The Sirian High Council

Many millions of years ago, the great Founder metaterrestrial races from the highest realms in the universe created a grand plan to seed many races and worlds throughout the cosmos. These magnificent beings are direct emanations of God Source, known as the cosmic trinity, and are Solar Body expressions located outside of space, time, and matter. One could say that God created these Ascended Master Beings as extensions of itself and assigned them the directive to go forth and create everything else. The goal of this creation endeavor was for all the created parts to return to God.

The intent of these universal architects was to contribute their most advanced genetic material in the creation of the First World, called Tara, better known as planet Earth, but existing in the 5th dimension. They would also create the magnificent inhabitants of this first world, the predecessors of the modern human being.

To oversee the creation of the First World, the Universal Founders first created a race to seed their consciousness through on Tara, and this very advanced race is the Lyrans, which utilized the genetic library of the metaterrestrials themselves.

The Lyrans created another subrace called the Elohim to oversee Lyran-Sirian genetic projects on Tara, while the Sirian Council was appointed by the Lyrans to manage these seedings.

The intricate biological blueprint of the root race seeding plan entailed the deliberate seeding of seven angelic root races and their corresponding subraces over time. These diverse genetic strains were drawn from the illustrious lineage of the 12 Essene Tribes, collectively constituting the rich tapestry of the human gene pool. The ultimate objective of this adapted plan was to guide each root race in the assembly of a specific DNA strand, a transformative process poised to elevate the collective human experience back to its origin within the highest echelons of existence. All of the knowledge of the universal founders would be genetically encoded into the DNA of these 12 divine tribes.

This intricate evolutionary seeding plan unfolded in the higher dimensions, with Planet Tara serving as the original abode of god-like humans meticulously crafted to safeguard the Universal Genetic Library.

Nevertheless, This grand plan by the creators to seed the human root races faced substantial challenges and setbacks even from its inception. The creation of the divine human and its various root race forms became one of the most contentious endeavors in the universe's history, eliciting strong opposition from the fallen races. They harbored a deep animosity toward the angelic human being, driven by their unattainable envy of the divine spark it possessed.

Numerous significant conflicts unfolded, spanning galactic and Earthly realms throughout the ages in response to this divine human creation. While these conflicts did disrupt the root race seeding process, the divine human being always overcame these challenges. Without fail, individuals from each root race seeding consistently managed to carry forward the next DNA strand of human evolution.

As the ages passed, it was time for Root Race 4 to emerge. It was a new day and time, and the grand creators were full of hope and excitement. In this fresh era, a golden age had just dawned as the Pleiadians and the Priesthood of UR, of the universal Melchizedek lineage, joined forces with the Lyran-Sirians in the unfolding grand seeding plan of the shining root race of the Atlanteans. These creators envisioned the Atlanteans as the most advanced human race to date, and their civilization was imbued with incredible technology, abilities, and wisdom.

The cities of Atlantis were built from celestial blueprints from the higher dimensions. Imagine majestic 5th-dimensional Atlantean cities all across the globe, where the boundaries between technology and nature blur into a seamless harmony. In great Atlantis, sublime beauty graced every corner, where architecture and geometry converge to create temples of unmatched splendor. Towering pyramids inlaid with crystal, gold, and silver, and intricate labyrinths stood as monuments to human ingenuity, while lush, life-giving landscapes stretched as far as the eye could see.

In this advanced civilization, the very essence of knowledge permeated the ether, illuminating the minds of its inhabitants. In this magical world, super-advanced technology coexisted with the natural world's rhythms, creating a symphony of progress and reverence.

Atlantis, constructed as a sacred realm on Earth, pushed the boundaries of possibility to their limits, representing the pinnacle of human accomplishment. Its majesty and advancement continue to evoke awe and wonder even in the present era.

During the creation of Atlantis, The Sirian Council upgraded the original root race seeding plan, and the mission's purpose shifted from being a simple genetic endeavor to a more profound mission centered around liberating and aiding the souls affected by the challenges faced during the first three root race seedings, which had resulted in changes to human DNA. This updated plan focused on the healing and restoration of the DNA, bringing it back to its original pristine condition.

To achieve this enhanced root race seeding plan, the High Council decided to embody the entirety of the Emerald Founders' Records in the DNA of the Atlantean beings and within the architecture and society of the civilization of Great Atlantis itself. The founders knew that future seeded races would need to acquire the knowledge within the founders' records before their DNA could be restored and their evolutionary journey could succeed.

And so Atlantis was created as a magnificent living library known as "The Emerald Library" that contained the full knowledge within the Emerald Founder Records that originated in the higher realms. This knowledge was highly protected and guarded, and all Atlanteans had the free will option and opportunity to advance their personal consciousness growth and ascension through the study and examination of these

Emerald Founder Records in the Atlantean Mystery Schools.

The Emerald Records are 12 holographic disc records crafted from selenite quartz crystals. These discs, created in Sirius B, house the evolutionary history of life within the Universal Time Matrix. Initially sourced from the Cosmic Hall of Records, they bear the Teachings of the Universal Melchizedek Lineages of the God worlds in the highest dimensions.

Within the Emerald Founder Records lies explicit knowledge concerning the origins, genetics, and purpose of the human race, including historical timeline accounts of Galactic history, considered the divine birthright of all angelic humans. These discs also contain highly advanced technological information and mathematical code for all universal processes, inner workings of the galactic and planetary stargates, and Ley Lines, as well as spiritual-science texts rooted in the Law of One consciousness freedom teachings, which unite sacred sciences with spirituality.

While many are familiar with The Emerald Tablets of Thoth, and though this is directly related, we discuss the difference in Chapter 7.

The island of Poseida, the capital city of Atlantis, housed most of the Atlantean schools of higher wisdom and was home to the Temple of One, the Temple of Healing, and the Temple of Knowledge. Its city was constructed of a series of walls and was encircled by flowing canals. It was an exquisite marvel of architecture, culture, and engineering. Poseida served as the central hub for the Crystalline power grid, housing the most exquisite Crystals in its vicinity. These remarkable Crystals were interlinked beneath a dome that could adjust its angle, allowing it to harness stellar, solar, and gravitational energy waves. A massive 50-foot translucent emerald-green crystal was placed in the center of the dome, causing the Isle of Poseida to exude an exquisite emerald-green aura that could be seen for miles. The magnificent and vibrant emerald crystal positioned at the dome's heart symbolized the Emerald Order's teachings from the highest dimensions. This bestowed upon Atlantis the title of the "Emerald Library," while Poseida, known as the Emerald City, stood as the most exquisite metropolis ever on Earth.

The great Library of Alexandria in Egypt was the last significant library on Earth connected to the Emerald Library of Atlantis. Later, Alexandria served as the repository for recording knowledge about Universal Laws, higher teachings, and accurate ancient history, as translated from and found in manuscripts from Emerald Founder Records. In the ancient world, Alexandria stood as the capital of knowledge and true learning, directly modeled after those who still remembered the great libraries and educational centers that had existed long before in the Atlantean Colonies. The fallen races have continuously sought to conceal the sacred knowledge within the Emerald Records, and the burning of the Library of Alexandria is a notable instance. Nonetheless, the wisdom persists.

Chapter 2: **Secrets of Atlantis**
The Sacred Sciences

"Knowledge is the foundation upon which the temple of wisdom is built, and in its light, we find our way back home. '

The Atlanteans

The Emerald Records, stored within the grand civilization of Atlantis, contained a wealth of universal and advanced knowledge about many subjects. This valuable information became the most sought-after knowledge in the universe.

The infusion of sacred sciences and technologies into the grandeur of Great Atlantis is nothing short of awe-inspiring. Each of these otherworldly advanced technologies finds its origins within the sacred Emerald Founder Records.

Ancient Builder Technology

The structures that formed the foundation of the global Atlantean empire are truly awe-inspiring marvels; many still stand on Earth today. Their creation becomes even more astonishing when we delve into the mysteries of Ancient Builder Technology. This knowledge, drawn from the Emerald Founder records, transports us to an era where human ingenuity reached unparalleled heights. Ancient Builder Technology is today a testament to the pinnacle of architectural achievement and technological innovation in human history. Even in the modern world, nothing of this magnitude has ever been constructed, and the methods behind it remain hidden, eluding complete understanding.

Picture the audacious choreography of handling colossal stone structures, some weighing several thousands of tons, executed with a precision that defies all modern methods. Cutting, transporting, placing, and finishing these massive stones to construct buildings was not a mere display of brute force; rather, it showcased a profound understanding of ancient and highly advanced building technology. The builder races meticulously aligned the structures with the stars, achieving extraordinary precision and crafting otherworldly masterpieces in Atlantis. Remarkable precision was applied in stone carving and polishing, leaving behind etched diamond blade cut marks on the very stones they shaped, indicating the use of advanced power sources and machine tools. Many of these ancient megalithic stones scattered across the planet today exhibit signs of having been softened or melted, and there is evidence of the stones being molded like blocks of ancient concrete.

The ancient teachings suggest that the Lyran-Sirian builder races employed large, powerful, advanced machines fueled by zero-point energy and crystal power. They combined this technological prowess with a profound metaphysical understanding of harnessing and manipulating natural forces to construct these megalithic structures.

The structures of great Atlantis were also intricately fused with the natural landscape. Every stone, every column, and every arch was not only a feat of engineering but also a work of art that melded seamlessly with the surrounding environment. Nature's geometry, so perfect in its design, became an integral part of these structures, enhancing their beauty and mystical allure. In addition, elegant crystals, gold, and silver were inlaid into the structures with a masterful touch. These precious elements didn't just serve as embellishments; they were harmoniously integrated into the design and its energy, amplifying these architectural wonders' spiritual and aesthetic significance.

These monumental structures are more than mere monuments; they are living testaments to the fusion of human vision, the natural world, and the divine.

Within the structures of Atlantis, we witness the manifestation of the timeless principle: 'As above, so below.' This profound saying, rooted in the original Emerald records, is key to understanding how the Sirian builders duplicated their higher-dimensional divine consciousness on Earth. In Atlantis, the grandeur of the cosmos was mirrored in the beauty and precision of these megalithic structures—a testament to the eternal dance between the earthly and the divine.

Stargate and Portal Technology

The Atlanteans, inheritors of the profound Emerald Founder records, developed astonishing Stargate technology as a pinnacle of their celestial mastery. These remarkable devices, gateways to the cosmos, enabled instantaneous travel across dimensions within the Holographic Time Matrix. Such mastery provided Atlanteans the key to traverse the stars and delve into the infinite tapestry of existence.

Simultaneously, the Atlanteans' understanding of cosmic portals further augmented this journey. They recognized these portals as natural, spiraling electromagnetic doorways interlinking various locations, dimensions, times, and parallel universes, offering diverse paths through the Dimensional Holographic Time Matrix.

The Atlanteans understood these cosmic gateways from The Emerald Founders Records. The stargates operated using the concept of the 12 Tree Grid, a foundational template for creation, symbolizing the Stargates as living portals. Moreover, Atlantean knowledge extended to Earth's energy anatomy, encompassing precise geographical coordinates of Chakras, Axiatonal Lines, Ley Lines, and energy vortices integral to the Planetary Auric Body. This understanding was critical in grasping how these cosmic portals and Stargates interacted with the very fabric of planetary consciousness, influencing diverse realities and the passage of time.

The Planetary Chakra system, often viewed as Stargates played a pivotal role in this perception of energy. These celestial gateways acted as intermediaries, channeling higher energies from the Source field through the Sun into various Stargates. Each gateway transmitted unique energy frequencies, forming bridges between higher and lower dimensions, and constituting an intricate energy cycle.

Atlantean grid workers, known as Templars, adept in interacting with Earth's holographic structures, unraveled the profound secrets of the planet's consciousness. They discovered Earth's reservoir of collective consciousness, stemming from the Grail Point within the planet's second-dimensional Stargates, a critical component in their understanding of cosmic and planetary dynamics. The sacred teachings further reveal that when DNA coding matches the frequency of a specific stargate, passage is allowed to higher dimensions.

DNA and Life Creation Sciences

The Atlanteans, enlightened by the Lyran-Sirian Races directly from the Emerald Founder recortaughtds, profoundly understood human DNA's intricacies. They knew the original human DNA imprint as the Silicate Matrix, a twelve-strand DNA template designed through dimensionalized mathematical programs.

The Atlantean scholars recognized that each segment of this Silicate Matrix corresponded to a DNA strand, intricately woven with 12 base magnetic female codes and 12 base-electrical male acceleration codes. These 24 codes formed a set of 12 Vector Codes. Each Vector Code, a specific coordinate within a timeline or grid network, was essential for activating the human DNA.

These 12 Vector Codes manifested in the human genome as 12 nucleotides, forming the nucleotide base pairs of the DNA strands. Each DNA strand corresponds to a Fire Letter or Fire Code, built upon electromagnetic impulses of sound arranged in patterned sequences. Every Fire Letter was linked to a dimensional frequency band of consciousness in the Universal Tree of Life or the 12 Tree Grid, and collectively, all Fire Letter Code sequences made up the 12-strand matrix, the original genetic construction code of the human species.

The Atlanteans viewed DNA not just as biological molecules but as miniaturized, crystallized frequencies - patterns of electromagnetic light that magnetically grouped into crystalline DNA Seed Codes. Each DNA strand, a conduit for a specific dimensional frequency band of consciousness, was a reflection of these Seed Codes, each composed of 12 magnetic particle units and 12 electrical anti-particle units.

The assembly level of an individual's DNA strands was determined by the frequency bands integrated into their Morphogenetic Field. The Atlanteans understood that as a person pulled in more frequency bands from the dimensional Unified Fields, their personal frequency accretion level rose, enabling more DNA codes to assemble and activate. The Atlanteans understood that DNA coding is the secret key that unlocks portal technology, allowing one to step across dimensions.

Reality Creation: Energy into Matter

The Atlanteans were known to be masters of reality creation, possessing profound knowledge in the art of materializing matter from energy. Their understanding, deeply rooted in the principles of quantum physics and derived from the Emerald Records, revealed the extraordinary ability to manifest anything instantaneously, guided by the focus of their energy and consciousness.

The Atlanteans comprehended that energy and matter were not separate entities at the quantum level but interconnected aspects of the same universal fabric. They believed the entire universe was a field of potentiality where energy, through focused intent and consciousness, could coalesce into matter. This process of energy materialization was not merely a theoretical concept but a practical application in their daily lives.

The Atlanteans learned from the original mystery school teachings that reality was shaped by where they directed their energy and attention. They understood that thoughts and intentions were not abstract, ephemeral phenomena but tangible forces interacting with the quantum field to shape physical reality. Directing their consciousness with precise intent could influence the quantum field to manifest their desired outcomes.

This mastery of reality creation was more than just an ability to bring forth objects or fulfill material needs; it was a profound expression of their deep alignment with the universal laws of creation embodied in the Law of One. The Atlanteans knew that the universe responded to their thoughts and the vibrational frequency of their emotions and beliefs. By maintaining a state of high vibrational frequency, characterized by positive emotions and thoughts, they could materialize their intentions faster and more effectively.

Free Energy

Energy, in its essence, is about consciousness, a concept deeply understood in the advanced civilization of Atlantis. The Atlanteans mastered the Emerald Founder's concept of Zero Point Energy, also known as free energy, seeing it as an infinite source of power intrinsically linked to the universe's consciousness. This Zero Point God Matrix Field, radiating through the

Cosmic Trinity, gave rise to a multidimensional spectrum of life force and power across time and space. It was perceived as the boundless energy source of the Creator, present within all systems, harmoniously uniting the notions of divine energy, power, and authority.

Zero Point Energy, omnipresent and inexhaustible, was harnessed through sophisticated Atlantean technology. The Atlanteans realized that this energy, abundant in the space vacuum, offered limitless power potential. Their energy systems were based on the principle of Negentropy, contrasting sharply with Entropy. Negentropy symbolized the continuous replenishment and organization of energy, essential for their civilization's sustainable and balanced functioning.

To tap into this boundless source, the Atlanteans utilized Quartz Seed Crystals. These crystals, known for their unique properties, were adept at accessing and channeling the vast energy. This led to the realization that even the smallest spaces contained enough energy to power large cities sustainably.

The Atlanteans' understanding of free energy was more than just a technological advancement; it was a philosophy of living in harmony with the cosmos. It involved utilizing the natural order of the universe to sustain and enrich life. The principles of Negentropy, the Zero Point God Matrix Field, and the use of crystalline technology were all integral to their sophisticated understanding of free energy.

In the modern world, Nikola Tesla re-discovered this infinite free energy source and referred to it as scalar or radiant energy from the ether.

Some general properties of scalar waves include:
1. Travel faster than the speed of light.
2. It seems to transcend space and time.
3. Cause the molecular structure of water to become coherently reordered.
4. Positively increases immune function in mammals.
5. They are involved in the formation process in nature.

Matter Transformation: Alchemy

In the advanced civilization of Atlantis, the practice of alchemy and transformation was a highly revered science. This ancient art, often misconceived as solely the transformation of base metals like lead into precious metals like gold, was a sophisticated process involving intricate manipulation of the elemental properties of matter. The Atlanteans could transform any element of matter into any other!

With their profound understanding of the natural world, the Atlanteans knew that all matter was composed of basic building blocks, which could be rearranged and transformed through alchemical processes. They understood that by altering the energetic and atomic structure of a substance, they could transmute it into a completely different form. This concept went beyond mere metaphor; it was a practical application of their deep knowledge of matter at its most fundamental level.

In their alchemical endeavors, the Atlanteans focused on manipulating what they termed 'Prima Materia' or the 'first matter.' This Prima Materia was considered the raw, unformed substance from which all matter could be derived. The process of transmutation involves breaking down a substance to its primal form and then reconstructing it into a new form. The

Atlanteans mastered this process, not just in theory but in practice, applying it to various elements and compounds.

The Atlantean alchemists were adept at controlling the process of matter transmutation through precise techniques. They utilized unique catalysts, often derived from rare minerals or specific crystalline structures, to initiate and direct the transmutation process. They also employed specific chants or vibrational sounds, which helped align the energetic frequencies of the materials involved, facilitating the transformation.

The process was not simple nor arbitrary; it required a deep understanding of the properties of the elements involved, how to break them down to their Prima Materia state, and the conditions necessary for their transformation. For instance, turning lead into gold wasn't just a matter of applying heat or mixing chemicals; it involved a complex procedure of altering the atomic structure of lead, which the Atlanteans achieved through a combination of chemical, energetic, and even psychic processes.

Monatomic Gold

Monatomic Gold, known as the 'Philosopher's Stone' in Atlantean alchemy and recorded in the mysterious Emerald Founder records, held a special place in Atlantean culture. This remarkable substance exceeded earthly value, possessing properties that defied our understanding. In Atlantis, Monatomic Gold was more than a precious metal; it served as a gateway to spiritual insight, expanded consciousness, and journeys into other dimensions.

The Atlanteans used Monatomic Gold to explore profound spiritual realms and venture beyond the physical world. It played a vital role in their quest for enlightenment, helping them connect with higher planes and unlocking hidden potentials within the human spirit. Monatomic Gold acted as a portal to uncharted territories of consciousness, offering experiences beyond the limits of the material realm.

The influence of Monatomic Gold extended beyond Atlantis, leaving its mark on later cultures. In ancient Egypt, Monatomic Gold took the form of 'White Powder or Manna Cakes,' which enhanced and prolonged the life of Egyptian royals. These cakes were closely tied to the gods and the journey to the afterlife, earning them the name 'Bread of Long Life.'

Drawing inspiration from Atlantean alchemy, the Egyptians considered these White Manna Cakes sacred offerings that bridged the mortal realm with the divine. They were seen as a way to purify the body and soul, facilitating a deeper connection with the spiritual dimensions and aiding in the ascension process beyond the physical plane.

It's important to note that while Monatomic Gold enhances DNA and promotes long cellular life, it cannot replace true organic immortality, which comes only from being connected to source energy.

Atlantean Pyramid And The Arc Of The Covenant

The Lyran-Sirian builder races meticulously constructed expansive and highly advanced pyramids within Atlantis and the region of Giza, which was an integral part of the Atlantean empire. These pyramids were designed as stargate portals and placed on powerful Earth energy centers, serving as conduits to higher planes of existence.

The Great Pyramid of Giza originally contained the Arc of the Covenant Time Portal Passage and Machinery. The Giza Stargate is the site of the 4th-dimensional planetary stargate and was a location of both an architectural marvel and profound geographical significance, as it marked the Earth's center.

The Arc of the Covenant, as understood in Atlantean times, was far more than a religious artifact; it was a time portal passage between Earth and the Andromeda galaxy. Created 840,000 years ago by Guardian Races, this portal was part of the highly advanced technology of the Ancient Builder Races. The Arc of the Covenant, along with its network interfaces of Stargates and more, was integrated into the planetary system. This Arc was a portal bridge that spans multiple dimensional frequency spectrums and connects different time and space locations between Earth and Andromeda. Its function extended beyond mere transportation; it was designed for genetic rehabilitation, aiming to reset the divine blueprint for healing the soul, monad, and Avatar crystal body per the original angelic human being template.

This understanding of the Atlantean Stargate and the Master Pyramid, derived from the knowledge in the Emerald Founder records, showcased the Atlanteans' advanced grasp of cosmic and interdimensional travel, blending architectural mastery with profound technological and spiritual insights.

Halls of Amenti

The Halls, or Sphere of Amenti, is a time portal passage that holds the race blueprint of humanity. These sacred Halls, situated in the depths of inner Earth below Giza, comprise six portals that enable dimensional exploration, liberating individuals from the confines of the 3D Earth system. Journeying through these Halls, one can access, review, and reconstruct memories and events, helping them rediscover the path that leads back to their divine origin.

Within these hallowed Halls, monumental holographic books conceal all information about human history and the recorded tapestry of the past. These books are also known as The Hall of Records and the Akashic Records.

Seekers within the mystery schools can begin their quest for wisdom within the grand halls; however, access to the halls is not freely granted. Earning entry requires the sincere exploration of one's soul or demonstrating unwavering purity, moral character, and a steadfast commitment to one's soul's purpose throughout lifetimes. When access is granted by the Guardian Priests, the adept will discover pages that resonate with the echoes of their current lives and life missions, where each soul's blueprint is elegantly inscribed within these ethereal volumes.

The Egyptians were the last to know about the Halls of Amenti and the Sphere of Amenti's role in preserving the morphogenetic imprint for all Angelic Human tribes. Later, they safeguarded this ancient knowledge after the grid networks and records were lost during the Atlantean Cataclysm.

Atlantis, a civilization immortalized in the Emerald Founder records, epitomized the pinnacle of a high-tech society, featuring advanced technologies and power systems that far exceeded the standards of their time. Some of these general technologies featured in Atlantis were:

Flight and Aerial Transportation: In Atlantis, the concept of flight took on a new dimension with advanced aircraft and anti-gravity vehicles. Combining aerodynamic design with sophisticated propulsion systems, these machines facilitated swift and efficient travel across great distances, transforming the Atlantean skies into a network of advanced aerial pathways.

Ground and Maritime Transportation: Atlantean transportation technologies were equally innovative on land and sea. Ground vehicles and maritime vessels were powered by advanced energy systems, enabling high-speed and environmentally friendly travel. Their maritime technology, in particular, allowed for seamless navigation in the depths of the oceans and across vast expanses of water.

Communication and Information Technology: Atlantis also boasted advanced telecommunication systems, allowing instantaneous information exchange over long distances. Their knowledge storage and retrieval methods, possibly utilizing crystal-based technologies, were highly advanced, capable of storing vast amounts of information in efficient and compact forms.

In the great civilization of Atlantis, all of these remarkable advanced technologies were part of daily life. However, amidst these astonishing innovations, one stood out in Atlantean society: the crystals, particularly the Atlantean Master Crystals.

Chapter 3: **Atlantean Master Crystals**
Harnessing Divine Power

" In a crystal, we have clear evidence of the existence of a formative life principle, and though we cannot understand the life of a crystal, it is nonetheless a living being. "

Nikola Tesla

As a Starseed, you are most likely deeply drawn to the magic of Atlantis and Earth's crystals, as you hold powerful memories from the ancient days of that magnificent civilization. The energies left behind from those times still resonate within you, etched into your very being.

You may recall some of your magnificent work in great Atlantis:
- Working on your ascension.
- Serving in grand temples as a scientist/priest.
- Collaborating with souls you are close to today.

- Utilizing the natural energy of Earth and majestic crystals.
- Experiencing a great catastrophe that cut short your work.
- Attempting to save crucial information and technology.

It is time to reacquaint yourselves with your ancient higher selves and the profound knowledge of advanced crystal technology you possessed in ancient Atlantis. This knowledge was used for healing, ascension, transformation, and the foundation of various exotic technologies.

Long ago, you lived and walked among the gods of Earth in the golden civilization of Atlantis. Within this shining civilization, you guided this planet with advanced crystal knowledge and technology.

Your primary city, Poseida, located within the original 5-ringed city of Atlantis, held powerful vortex portals, including the temple of healing, the temple of sound, the temple of one, the temple of regeneration, and the temple of knowledge. You may have clear memories of working and living in these magnificent crystal temples.

The primary cities and temples of Atlantis featured 13 magnificent Atlantean master crystals. They were created using Sirian, Arcturian, and Pleiadian technology that was nothing short of other-worldly.

The 13 Atlantean Master Crystals were awe-inspiring crystals of radiant beauty and immense size, standing approximately 20 feet wide and 50 feet tall. They appeared as magnificent translucent and shining colored blocks, reflecting the vibrant hues of the rainbow. Each master crystal emitted a captivating-colored aura that extended for miles, illuminating the surroundings with their divine radiance. Their presence mesmerized and filled the ancient Atlanteans with a profound sense of wonder and spiritual energy.

Each master crystal was carefully positioned within the heart of key infrastructure, such as advanced technology centers, healing chambers, and communication hubs. This crystal was ingeniously incorporated into the intricate architecture of Atlantis. All buildings and structures in those ancient days were constructed with these beautiful crystals as integral design elements, emitting sublime pastel colors and radiant light.

The Master Crystals were power generators to energize the city's advanced machinery, transportation systems, and crystal-powered vehicles. Colored light emitted by the master crystals served as an efficient communication system, enabling instantaneous transmission of information across vast distances. The mesmerizing vibrations of the crystals also contributed to a harmonious and elevated state of consciousness among the Atlantean populace, fostering spiritual development and collective unity. These technological marvels empowered Atlantis to thrive as an advanced civilization, guided by the wisdom of the Atlantean master crystals and their capacity to channel and harness cosmic energies.

In the advanced civilization of Atlantis, the 13 Atlantean Master Crystals played a pivotal role in energizing and powering essential aspects of society. These magnificent crystals harnessed superconducting lattice properties, converting any type of energy from one form to another. Also, just like modern electronic devices, these crystals could receive, store, transmit, and amplify energies.

In great Atlantis, the remarkable ability to harness crystal energy was a defining aspect of their advanced civilization. Beyond their practical uses, these crystals were integral to the Atlanteans' more esoteric endeavors, including Stargate and ascension technologies, and serving as mediums for data storage and energy grid work.

Even more astounding was the Atlanteans' use of these master crystals for healing and promoting longevity in the human body. Atlantis was renowned for its exceptional healing technologies, where advanced medical devices incorporating crystal energy were used for rejuvenation and healing. Guided by the Emerald Founder Records, The Atlanteans had a profound understanding of human anatomy and were skilled in treating various ailments. This extensive knowledge, coupled with their sophisticated technology, contributed significantly to their extended lifespans. The seamless integration of crystal energy in medical applications highlighted their blend of scientific advancement and holistic wisdom.

In Atlantis, an elaborate network of massive scalar healing crystals was central to the sacred healing temples. These crystals, precisely attuned to the human body's vibrational frequencies, acted as potent energy amplifiers and conductors. Surrounding these magnificent crystals, individuals experienced harmonic oscillations that stimulated the body's natural healing mechanisms, fostering holistic well-being.

These enormous crystals, cut with exacting precision to a phi ratio, emitted scalar energy, known for their profound healing effects on the human body. The crystals amplified and focused this energy, facilitating miraculous healing within minutes. This scalar energy, reaching deep into the body's energy centers and cellular matrix, restored balance and alignment and could even regenerate damaged tissues, challenging conventional healing paradigms.

These ancient healing chambers, utilizing technology similar to modern holographic med-bed technology, leveraged scalar energy in ways that are only now being rediscovered.

The 13 Atlantean master crystals were not merely quartz crystals but an extraordinary fusion of quartz, other crystals, and natural glass. They also contained gold, silver, platinum, diamond, and beryl traces. Within their sublime structure, these crystals also contained something special: monatomic elements, granting them unparalleled technical prowess and capabilities. In modern times, high-spin monatomic elements are linked to superconductors that challenge the laws of physics. In scientific tests, they have demonstrated the ability to defy gravity and the laws of mass and weight, possess zero-point energy capabilities, and transcend time and space.

The sublime beauty and potent essence of these divine crystals continue to resonate within the psyche of modern descendants of Atlantis on earth today. In modern times, the concept of these crystals is widely recognized as Andara Crystals. While authentic versions of these crystals are rare today due to their deep location inside the earth, special mining operations can produce them just as diamonds are mined. Many have been found in kimberlite mines in the Sierra Nevada mountains, where the secondary ancient Atlantean mining operation was located.

One application for an Andara crystal is to serve as a crystal amplifier. This unique quality becomes evident when the crystal is placed near the human auric field. The Andara crystal operates by receiving light from a higher dimensional source, effectively storing this energy, and then projecting it outward in a significantly amplified form. The process of manifesting in the material world from the energetic realm is greatly enhanced in the presence of an Andara crystal. The Andara Crystal acts as a powerful catalyst by utilizing well-known manifestation techniques such as visualization and deeply feeling and experiencing the presence of a desired outcome in the current moment. Its presence markedly boosts the manifestation process, often yielding surprisingly quick and effective results, demonstrating its potent ability to enhance and transform energetic intentions into tangible realities.

Throughout history, the legends of these majestic master crystals have endured, and their memory continues to evoke a sense of reverence and fascination among those who hear their stories. They have been called the "grail stones" and the "fire stones," as their legacy remains imprinted in the collective memory of humanity as symbols of divine beauty, wisdom, and illumination.

According to ancient Atla-ra Priesthood teachings, the primary ringed city of Atlantis was not located thousands of miles from the east coast of America but was directly connected to the land of the Americas' east coast before the great deluge rearranged the Atlantic ocean. The land of America, in general, was also part of Atlantis, and right in the middle of the continent, where modern-day Arkansas now sits, was the primary Atlantean crystal seeding and mining operation. The energy vortex in this region, created by ley lines, drew the Atlanteans to the area, where they utilized advanced Pleiadian and Arcturian technology to seed and grow powerful crystals, some weighing up to 100 tons.

Approximately 13,000 years ago, before the great calamity approached, you, as members of the Atla-ra priesthood, took measures to save the knowledge and the crystals. Weeks before the catastrophe, you placed the Atlantean master crystals deep under the ground and locked them with a dimensional seal for protection in Arkansas, Brazil, Mount Shasta, Bimini, and lake

Titicaca. In modern times, still buried under 6 miles of sediment, beneath these sacred sites, lie the ancient Atlantean crystals, which have lain dormant for over 13,000 years.

These master crystals, programmed and coded by the benevolent scientist priests of atla-ra, are awakening again in modern times and will play an important role in the current ascension cycle. The surge of energy from these crystals synergizes with planned coding enhancements, resulting in an unparalleled transformation of the crystalline energies within the earth. As your innate understanding of Atlantean crystal technology awakens, you will lead humanity to harness the potent energies in these sacred locations.

As you awaken further, you shall remember the full knowledge of crystal technology and learn to manipulate matter, space, and time. With their powerful harmonic energy, the crystals themselves assist you in elevating your vibration, reconnecting you as the grand keeper of the sacred grail stones of Atlantis.

Chapter 4: **The Battle for Earth**
Light vs. Darkness

" The light shines in the darkness, and the darkness has not overcome it."

John The Prophet

Since time immemorial, the forces of darkness have conflicted with the forces of light across the cosmos. In this vast cosmic struggle, a key focus lies on controlling the stargates within the holographic dimensional matrix. It's widely understood that whoever commands these stargates gains significant influence over the entire cosmos.

Parallel to this, there is a considerable effort by the fallen races to undermine the human race, primarily driven by their envy of the unique divine spark within humanity. This spark, representing immense potential and power, positions humans as significant figures in this age-old cosmic contest.

As you read this chapter, remember that the history of the cosmos and humankind is a story woven with light and darkness, reflecting the balance and interplay of yin and yang.

It's crucial for those who embrace the light to recognize that existence is not solely composed of love and light. Acknowledging that we harbor light and dark aspects together to form a complete whole is essential. We leave ourselves incomplete when we try to ignore or reject our darker side. Only by embracing, understanding, and working with our darkness can we transmute and heal it, achieving a state of true wholeness. Remember, harmonizing the dark and light aspects to balance the polarity back to zero-point is crucial to the cosmic ascension plan.

The Guardian teachings, sourced from the Emerald Founder records and imparted in the mystery schools of Atlantis and Egypt within the original blue flame Melchizedek Essene priesthood, offer an honest and truthful account of galactic and Earth history.

These teachings recount the galactic battles of the past and clearly distinguish between the forces of good and evil, providing a deeper understanding of the key players in our history. They reveal the distorted narratives propagated by various groups, clarifying who the 'good guys' and 'bad guys' are. As you delve deeper into these teachings, be prepared for surprises and a wealth of clarity and insight into these complex topics.

Be aware that part of the agenda of the fallen races, which seized control of Earth eons ago, was to obscure this knowledge and keep humanity uninformed. Comprehending the more challenging aspects of our history and the actions of the fallen races can initially feel overwhelming and appear somber for those aligned with the light. However, it's vital to remember that humanity has always persevered and will continue to triumph. Despite everything, humans stand resilient, as does our beloved planet Earth.

The guardian races overseeing this cosmic drama hold the keys to resolution. While they respect free will and the natural unfolding of the evolutionary plan, they have recently intervened significantly. They assure all beings that everyone finds their way back home, regardless of the challenges encountered on their journey.

There may be questions about how beings who have fallen, like those responsible for the destruction of Lyra, can exist within higher dimensions. The Founders' teachings suggest that negativity exists up to the 11th dimension in the Dimensional Holographic Time Matrix. Initially, within the higher dimensions, all beings were benevolent. However, as the Founders' Races seeded the first races, some began to experience shifts in their DNA, transforming into different races with varying attributes. These beings began to undergo convoluted DNA, initiating their descent from grace and falling downward from the 11th dimension.

Revealing the Principal Fallen Angelic Races of the Cosmos

Fallen Elohim Races of the Jehovian Family
- Jehovians: the Fallen Annu-Elohim
- Anunnaki: Jehovian-Anunnaki
- Nephilim: Egyptian-Anunnaki
- Annu: Annu-Melchizedeks, Urantia, Templar Annu, Illuminati

Fallen Seraphim Races

- Omicron or Dragon Moth: Insectoid-Dino-Reptiles
- Drakon: Dragons, Drakonian
- Draconis: Human-Lizard-Hominid
- Obedicrom: Avian-Reptile

Zeta Reticuli Races

- Zeta Reticulan Insectoid and Short Grays
- Zeta Rigelian Insectoid and Tall Grays

Fallen Annu-Drakon Hybrids

- Necromiton: Beetle-Human
- Men in Black: Human-Insectoid
- Vampire Serpent-Dino-Human
- Centaurs

Fallen Races of the Luciferian Family

- Enlil Anunnaki Hybrid Race: Scaled Reptile-Hominid
- Enki Anunnaki Hybrid Race: Insectoid-Reptile-Serpent
- Marduk Anunnaki Hybrid Race from the Satan Race Line.

Now, let's review the list of major galactic wars between the forces of light and dark from Lyra to Lemuria.

Lyran Wars, Orion Wars (20 Million Years Ago)

- Everything began in Lyra, including the first major galactic war. This era involved challenges and conflicts created by the first fallen races but also marked the emergence of new aspects of human consciousness. These DNA wars later extended to Orion, where a significant shift in human history occurred.

Electric Wars (5 Million Years Ago)

- The Electric Wars were a time of upheaval, primarily concerning the First Root Race. An important event known as the Wall in Time led to the separation of 12-strand DNA. This era also involved soul fragmentation across various timelines and missions to recover and reunite these fragments.

Thousand Years War (1 Million Years Ago)

- This era was marked by philosophical conflicts centered around the Law of One. It involved debates between those who focused on self-service and those who prioritized service to others. This time also saw the emergence of hybrid root races, such as the first Draco and Annu hybrids, and conflicts involving the Elohim and Anunnaki.

Nephilim Wars (75,000 Years Ago)

- During this period, there was an attempt to create the Nephilim through the Anunnaki Breeding Program, which was not accepted by the Elohim. Significant events included the Melchizedek and Annu DNA fractures, and the quarantine seal was placed around the solar system to protect human DNA.

Lemurian Holocaust (52,000 Years Ago)

- The Lemurian Holocaust represents the first major historical battle in the timeline of Earth. It was a time of complex interactions between light and dark, including a Draconian invasion of Lemuria through underground tunnels. This era also witnessed climatic changes, including the Ice Age, and surface-level environmental disruptions.

Following Lemuria, more battles ensued on planet Earth between the forces of darkness and light, and we will explore these in the upcoming chapters.

Chapter 5: **The Guardian Knights**
Defenders of Humanity

" A guardian angel, in its silent watch, is the sacred keeper of God's most precious treasure: the human soul."

The Essenes

One of the most honorable and important positions one can hold in all of existence is to be a protector of the divine knowledge of the universe.

The Emerald Founder Records, which embody the Sacred Law of One teachings, contain incredible secrets about the operation and history of the cosmos and were a gift from the universal founders to the 12 angelic tribes of the human race.

This divine knowledge was the principal spiritual teaching widely recognized during the Lemurian and early Atlantean timelines.

The Lyran-Sirian High Council bestowed an honorable and significant responsibility upon an esteemed group known as the Essenes, referred to as The Guardian Maji Priest Kings from the original Blue Ray Melchizedek line.

These Essene Priests, representing the 12 tribes, were entrusted with multifaceted responsibilities. One leader from each tribe was chosen to serve as the primary guardian of their tribe's planetary stargate. Simultaneously, they were tasked with translating the founders' records that detailed human historical timelines linked to the seeding of the 12 Tribes. They also held the sacred duty of transmitting this invaluable knowledge across multiple timelines, designating spiritually trained individuals to impart this wisdom to the 12 human tribes.

Many well-known spiritual groups, each with unique contributions, have been part of the Magi Grail Kings. These groups include the Essenes, who were known for their spiritual insights; the Salem Priests, with their ancient traditions; the Atla-Ra Priests, who had advanced wisdom; the Priesthood of UR, who upheld traditional customs, the Cathars, who championed purity and simplicity, the Druids and Celts connected to nature's mysteries, and the Gnostics who sought hidden knowledge. All of these groups were Christos Templars, which had their roots in the maternal lines of the Christos founders.

The roles of these Guardian Priests in great Atlantis extended beyond the preservation of wisdom down through history; they were instrumental in guiding and nurturing human spiritual evolution. As custodians of ancient teachings, they ensured this invaluable knowledge was preserved and passed down through generations. Though often in the background, their service has been a cornerstone in the evolution of human consciousness, bridging the celestial and Earthly realms with their wisdom, support, and care.

The Great Guardian Knights, guardians of divine knowledge, embodied the knight's code of honor and epitomized virtues like purity, generosity, and humility, essential for well-being and nurturing spiritual growth. They achieved personal freedom and ethical strength by fostering these virtues and replacing ego with heart-based devotion. Their commitment involved compassionate communication, self-compassion, and responsible actions, leading to a balanced life. Aligning with the Law of One in service to all, they embodied strong moral character and peaceful, spiritual living. They stood as luminaries, revered for their commitment to the greater good, placing humanity's well-being above their own. In an era where knowledge equated to power, these guardians were the vanguards against corruption, dedicated to nurturing an enlightened society. Their dedication, even to this day, ensures that this wisdom remains safe, ready to guide humanity back to its celestial heritage.

These spiritual leaders, organized in rainbow round tables within the Mystery Schools in great Atlantis, were more than mere guardians; they were the bearers of humanity's cosmic origins from the Emerald Records and the Law of One teachings. Their central mission revolved around disseminating this sacred knowledge in the Mystery Schools to expand humanity's consciousness, aligning with the Founders' Races divine evolutionary plan.

Throughout history, these Maji Priests have played a crucial role as guardians, knights, priests, and teachers of the Founder's knowledge. Above all, they were revered as exemplary angelic humans and great guardians of light.

Among the most notable and revered figures who were Maji Priests, several stand out for their profound spiritual depth and historical significance.

King Arthur, a symbol of chivalry and virtue, is a part of this group. He comes from the Fey bloodline, connected to Earth Guardians overseeing important timelines. The Cosmic Christ, represented by Cosmic Solar Dragons, is linked to Arthur's Pendragon or Fey Grail Bloodline. King Arthur protected the original Nazarene Teachings, preserved by the Celtic Church. His legends hold ancient memories of our origins in Lyra and Gaia.

The United Kingdom has a unique energy pattern, combining male and female aspects of the Maji Grail King's energy, tied to the 6th and 7th dimensions. This special energy operates within the Albion Lightbody, making it a powerful center for global awakening and shifting timelines. This awakening Albion is vital for transitioning to the Golden Age of Ascension in the next Harmonic Universe.

King Arthur's cosmic consciousness is closely linked to the Family of Michael of The Blue Flame, another familiar Maji Guardian protector of the 11th-dimensional gates of Aveyon-Avalon. Therefore, throughout history, King Arthur is considered a patriarch of the Archangel Michael avian genetics and Seraphim memories.

Jeshua, the most well-known Melchizedek Grail Templar, has impacted the world with his teachings of love and compassion. Guardian Yeshua, or Jesus the Christ, holds a special role as an anointed Cosmic Christos. He serves the purpose of reclaiming the Christos Mission and is an eternal Christos Solar Dragon King or Cosmic Dragon Starhuman who originated in the Seven Higher Heavens of the Andromeda Galaxy.

Guardian Yeshua and Mary Magdalene came to Earth from Sirius, originating from a future timeline. Yeshua's mission was to retrieve wisdom from the Founder Records, encompassing humanity's true origins and historical events like the Luciferian Rebellion and Atlantean Cataclysm. He conveyed this knowledge through written Gnostic texts to restore Inner Christos to humanity. Yeshua's Essene team, including his wife and twelve others, infused rainbow frequencies into Earth's ley lines. They utilized hidden portals in Egypt and Amarna to gather valuable knowledge and conceal advanced technology in the UK and Ireland. Their work involved realigning the planetary grid and stargate system, reversing the influence of fallen invaders, and preparing humanity for the Ascension Cycle. After his mission, Yeshua ascended from Earth with Guardian support.

When history speaks of those who made the most significant spiritual contributions to Earth, brought goodness, and defended humanity, it remembers these great guardians. They are the genuine guardian angels, protectors of humanity's spiritual essence.

In ancient Atlantis, before the great flood during the radiant era of the 4th root race, the Maji Grail Kings took on a sacred mission with unwavering dedication. Their goal was to create an unparalleled spiritual repository for timeless wisdom. Guided by the emerald records and fueled by their deep sense of purpose, these Priest Kings succeeded in founding Earth's most renowned scientific and spiritual library—the Atlantean Mystery Schools.

Chapter 6: **The Mystery Schools**
Portals to Wisdom

"Mystery is the key that unlocks the doors to the universe."

The Pleiadians

The Mystery Schools began on Earth in the heart of ancient Lemuria as the Great White Brotherhood Emerged, a time when the world was characterized by serenity and contemplation. Here, wisdom seekers gathered to delve into the depths of their inner selves, fostering the birth of these profound institutions. As the ages unfurled, the teachings of the Mystery Schools found their way to Atlantis, where they reached their zenith.

The Guardian priests and spiritual leaders of Atlantis, aware of the potent power of the Emerald Founder's knowledge, kept these schools secret to preserve the purity and potency of their teachings.

The primary aim of these mystery schools was to explore and understand the deeper mysteries of existence - life, death, and the cosmos. They sought to guide initiates towards gnosis, a profound spiritual awakening and understanding, allowing them a deeper comprehension of the universe and their role within it.

The teachings at these schools transcended academic knowledge. They were transformative, designed to elevate the initiate's inner being. Through a blend of meditation, ritualistic practices, and the study of sacred texts and symbols, initiates embarked on a spiritual awakening and self-discovery journey.

Atlantean teachings were rich in symbolism, drawing from the civilization's advanced understanding of the universe. Symbols were not just teaching tools but also encoded the profound secrets of their spiritual practices. These symbols had multiple layers, each revealing deeper truths as the initiate progressed on their spiritual path.

Initiation into the Atlantean Mystery Schools was a profound, life-altering process. It began with rigorous trials to test the readiness and worthiness of the candidate. Successful candidates then underwent initiation rites that symbolized a spiritual rebirth. These rituals, often held in sacred spaces filled with ancient symbolism, involved sacred chants and invocations, marking the transformation of the initiate into a spiritually enlightened being.

The Abydos temple of Egypt is one ancient Atlantean mystery school location still on Earth today. Abydos is a sacred institution whose origins are intertwined with Atlantis. Imagine walls within this ancient sanctuary, inscribed with cryptic hieroglyphics that whisper of futuristic vehicles and transcendental knowledge. These symbols are not mere art; they are keys to unlocking the connection between our world and realms beyond human comprehension. The temple chamber's hallowed grounds depicting spiritual figures' resurrection resonate with an almost tangible energy of hidden power and ancient wisdom, echoing the divine and powerful teachings hidden within.

Threefold Founder Flame

The Threefold Founder Flame is a central concept in universal creation, closely linked to the cosmic structure. It originates from three primal sound fields, forming the foundational rays of everything in our Universal Time Matrix. At its heart is the Solar Rishi, comprising three distinct orders: the Emerald Order with the Blue Flame, the Gold Order with the Gold Flame, and the Amethyst Order with the Violet Flame, known as the Universal Trinity or the Cosmic Trinity.

Each emanation has its significance:

1. Emerald Order - The First Emanation: The initial expression of the God Source, symbolizing a vital part of universal creation.
2. Gold Order - The Second Emanation: This expands the complexity of the universal structure.
3. Amethyst Order - The Third Emanation: Completes the fundamental triad of the Cosmic Trinity.

These orders, collectively known as the Founders or the Threefold Flame, form the (God Source Field) Triad, a living structure of sound-light universal consciousness called the Guardian Host.

The Three Universal Founder Rays – the Blue Ray Mother Arc, the Violet-Magenta Ray Father Arc, and the Golden Ray Sun of Christos – represent different dimensions of light: the Blue Flame in 13D, the Gold Flame in 14D, and the Violet Flame in 15D, constituting the Threefold Founder Flame. Think of each flame or order as a primary race blueprint, essentially a beginning collective or a family. Every race seeded within the Holographic Time Matrix stems from one of these three founding flames.

Adding to this cosmic narrative is the Aurora from the Seven Higher Heavens in Andromeda, who collaborate with the Guardian Host and bring in Omniversal God Sources, known as the Aurora Host, to assist humanity in their current ascension.

Understanding "God" in Cosmic Christos Guardian Perspective

The Cosmic Christos Guardians view "God" as transcending traditional religious interpretations. In this view, "God" is not a distinct personage but represents a profound, intrinsic concept. The true essence of God, the Inner Christos, is found within the Sacred Crystal Heart. Understanding "God" involves seeking truth and developing a pure heart and mind, supported by the Christos Guardian spirits.

Based on the Emerald Records and the Law of One, the concept of "God" is defined as:
- All That Is: The total existence.
- All-One: A state of complete unity.
- Divine Eternal Source: The everlasting divine origin.
- Infinite Creator: The boundless architect.
- Center Point of All-Union: The convergence core.
- Eternal Living Light of God: The perpetual divine radiance.
- Eternal Spiritual Being: The unending spiritual essence.
- Eternal Source of Intelligent Creation: The timeless source of conscious creation.
- Beloved Holy Presence: The sacred existence.
- Holy Mother, Holy Father, Holy Christos-Sophia: The divine aspects of creation.
- Love and Goodness.

The God-Sovereign-Free (GSF) Protocol

Per the founders' race protocols, all beings are considered God, sovereign, and free. The motto "God, Sovereign, Free (GSF)" embodies this belief. According to the Law of One, every being is a manifestation of God, or simply, 'all beings are God.' Since all beings are expressions of the singular divine essence, no being is superior to another, and each one is inherently God, Sovereign, and Free! Remember that even though some beings have rebelled against these divine principles and are considered fallen, they are still aspects of God. Similarly, some may not be conscious of their true nature, yet they, too, are embodiments of God.

The Cosmic Trinity of the Three Universal Founder Rays – Blue Ray Mother Arc, Magenta Ray Father Arc, and Golden Ray Sun of Christos – serve as the Guardian Host, protecting these spiritual liberation rights for all beings in the cosmos.

Achieving energetic balance through God, Sovereign, Free (GSF) Behaviors aligns us with our spiritual nature, fostering health, peace, and conscious development. Embracing the principle of "Kindness Above All" during the Ascension process, which emphasizes self-respect, healing, and extending kindness, nurtures our soul, and contributes positively to collective growth and experience.

The Law of One

The Law of One presents a profound understanding that underpins the fabric of our universe: all things are composed of intelligent energy and are integral to the All-One. This concept isn't just a philosophical idea; it's a Sacred Science that delves into the mechanics of Christ Consciousness and the Natural Laws that govern our Universal Creation. At the heart of the Law of One is the realization that Eternal Truth is synonymous with Eternal Love. This Eternal Love is the Infinite Creator's organic consciousness, often called God. When this consciousness of Eternal Love is embodied, it manifests as Unity intelligence, also recognized as the Inner Light of Christos. In harmony with God, this Unity consciousness ignites the Inner Light of Christos within us. Actualizing the Inner Light of Christos physically is related to embodying an Eternal God, a human. It is the physical manifestation of divinity, a reflection of the infinite in the finite. Practicing Unity Consciousness aligns with the image of God' s Love. This alignment brings us closer to our divine nature and ensures eternal protection. The Law of One teaches us that everything in the universe is interconnected through a singular divine source. By embracing this unity and recognizing the Eternal Love at the core of all existence, we can attain a state of oneness with the universe. This state of oneness transcends mere intellectual understanding; it is a profound experiential awareness that reshapes our perception of self and the cosmos, leading us toward a harmonious and enlightened existence.

The Law of Compassion, a core aspect of the Law of One, teaches that compassion towards others aligns us harmoniously with ourselves, God, and the universe. This law is foundational for Christ consciousness and Hieros Gamos, the inner unity of human and divine. In Atlantean teachings, this is symbolized by the White Robes of the One, representing the union with the divine and the embodiment of Cosmic Christ Consciousness. Hieros Gamos is the sacred marriage of the human being with the divine essence.

The Law of Intent is integral to the Law of One, emphasizing that our reality is shaped by our thoughts, intentions, and the energy behind them. This law suggests the absence of intent means no consent, aligning our actions with the Law of Resonance. These laws, including Intent, Consent, Authority, and Structure, impact our personal power and spiritual consciousness. The Law of Intent teaches that the collective energy of our thoughts and words is more powerful than the words themselves.

The Law of Consent, vital for personal autonomy, states that our thoughts and intentions define our consent, influencing ourselves and others. This law governs our vibrational resonance and is crucial in maintaining control over our mind, body, and spiritual consciousness. It affirms our right to self-determination and dictates that our body and consciousness respond only to our authority. Our thoughts and behaviors, resonating with specific energies, determine the authorities we empower.

The Universal Laws of Structure govern the energetic and physical realms. These laws, often hidden in secret orders, guide the construction of structures from the cosmos to individual contexts. They help in understanding and controlling the flow of energies within any structure. This law teaches that understanding the ego's internal structures is key to mastering control over one's mind, body, and spiritual consciousness. It highlights that all matter consists of vibrating energy, and the form of a structure influences its vibrational energy and transformation.

Here are **The Thirteen Primary Universal Laws** as derived from the Emerald Founders Records and the Law of One as taught in the Atlantean Mystery Schools:

1. Law of Mentalism

The Universal Law of Mentalism highlights that everything in existence stems from a mental state or belief system. It's linked to the Cosmic Sovereign Law of Unity, suggesting everything is interconnected through the Universal Mind or the consciousness of infinite intelligence. Mastery of this law is crucial for influencing all other Natural Laws, as our thoughts can affect outcomes across multiple dimensions.

2. Law of Correspondence

This law illustrates that our inner world reflects in our outer world, "as above, so below; as below, so above." It's about understanding the patterns of consciousness across different dimensions to gain insight into causal realities and events in our lives.

3. Law of Polarity

The Law of Polarity, or the Law of Opposites, indicates that everything has two sides or poles. Recognizing and understanding these opposites can elevate our perspective and help achieve balance by integrating these polarities within ourselves.

4. Law of Rhythm

This law teaches that there is a rhythmic motion between opposites, emphasizing that everything moves in specific rhythms or cycles. Recognizing these rhythms helps us maintain balance and navigate through changes.

5. Law of Suggestion

Suggestion shapes our thoughts, feelings, or behaviors. We need to focus on positive ideas and maintain a detached perspective to shift away from negative influences. Emotional clarity is key to overcoming fear-based suggestions.

6. Law of Response

This law tells us that seeking guidance from spiritual realms always brings a response, often through intuition or symbolic images. It embodies the Golden

Rule emphasizing treating others as one would like to be treated, a fundamental principle for ethical conduct.

7. Law of Cause and Effect

Every action has a corresponding reaction, with no randomness or luck involved. Positive actions lead to positive results, and vice versa. Understanding this law is crucial for taking responsibility for our actions and their energy.

8. Law of Transformation

Consciousness undergoes continuous transformation, moving from one form to another in an endless cycle. This transformation is part of spiritual growth and evolution, bringing us closer to enlightenment and transcendence.

9. Law of Transcendence

This law is experienced when we feel love as omnipresent and achieve an awakened consciousness. It involves co-creating with the God Source and deepens our understanding of our relationship with the Creator.

10. Law of Verification

Verification involves applying knowledge from life experiences to everyday situations. It encourages seeing challenges as opportunities for growth and testing our understanding of ourselves and our spiritual commitment.

11. Law of Cycles

The Law of Cycles governs the movement in the Wheel of Life, where consciousness journeys through time, encountering challenges and opportunities for growth. It emphasizes the perpetual cycle of change and renewal.

12. Law of Vibration

Everything in the universe vibrates at various speeds, forming different frequency rates. Understanding this law helps us realize that changing our thoughts can alter our mental state into a more positive, higher-vibrating one.

13. Law of Gender

This law covers the masculine and feminine principles essential for creation and regeneration. Understanding and harmonizing these gender principles is key to achieving Unity consciousness and spiritual healing.

When spiritual seekers are advised to adhere to the Laws of God, it means understanding how these divine universal laws influence all aspects of life and striving to live according to them to ensure a positively fulfilled life.

You may have noticed these Founder's principles, though similar to the teachings of the Emerald Tablets of Toth, have a very keen difference, which will be further explored in the upcoming chapter.

Chapter 7: **Whispers of Betrayal**
The Fall from Grace

"Light is information, and darkness is the lack of it!"

The Pleiadians

The story of Atlantis is complex and multifaceted, characterized by significant achievements and profound challenges. Once a pinnacle of advanced civilization, Atlantis attracted both awe and envy. As it rose to prominence, it became a target for destructive forces, leading to its eventual decline and fall.

While Atlantis was thriving as a pinnacle of advanced civilization, the Anunnaki were simultaneously expanding their influence on Earth. Initially, they began subtly encroaching upon and interfering with Atlantean society, gradually making their presence felt.

The Anunnaki, an 11th-dimensional fallen race, underwent a significant shift in their role on Earth during the Atlantean Era. Enki and Enlil orchestrated a devious plan to seize control of the entire solar system, including planet Earth. Their scheme threatened the integrity of human genetic makeup, driven by deep envy of the innate human potential and spiritual essence. This cosmic takeover plan would begin in Atlantis.

During this tumultuous time, Thoth, Enki's son and an esteemed entity from the 11th dimension, chose to side with his Anunnaki family. Previously loyal to the Christos Founders and a key figure in Atlantis's Melchizedek Mystery Schools, Thoth had access to sacred knowledge. However, he secretly played both sides, using his abilities to influence Earth's events for his own gain, aligning with the fallen Anunnaki, who sought global control.

Thoth's rise to power was driven by his belief in the Anunnaki's genetic superiority. Despite his significant impact on Earth, he remained a fallen being, far from a hero to humanity. Known also as Lucifer, Thoth was initially a respected light being. His desire for power and pride led him to turn against the light, betraying those allied with the Emerald Covenant and manipulating the truth for his own dark purposes. He was indeed known as the greatest double agent of all time. Moreover, the Luciferians' concealment of this cosmic-level espionage was so adept that most individuals remain oblivious to the reality surrounding Thoth even today.

The Guardian Races were initially unaware of Thoth's schemes in Atlantis, partly due to the previous galactic war that had disrupted communication with the higher realms. It was also later revealed that convincing AI clones of Thoth existed across multiple timelines, complicating the understanding of his true loyalties and actions. The Toth enigma has been called 'The Mystery of Mysteries' down through the ages by the forces of light.

Thoth and Enki, Enlil, and other Jehovian Anunnaki embodied the Luciferian archetype. They led the Luciferian Rebellion to dominate Earth during Atlantis's era. Marduk, Enki's later son, continued this lineage.

Enlil and Enki started the rebellion as their domination plan neared fruition, breaking the Emerald Covenant with the Guardians. Just before the Atlantean Flood, the Thothian Luciferians formed the Luciferian Covenant, aiming for total control over humanity. This dark alliance also included other fallen races, collectively known as the "Sons of Belial."

They planned to erase the sacred knowledge in the Emerald Founder Records and destroy evidence of Ancient Builder Technologies. They infiltrated Atlantean Mystery Schools, seized the Law of One and tribal knowledge, and aimed to use this information for control.

The Brotherhood of the Snake, led by the Thothian group, intended to twist the Founder Records into a fear-based narrative, enforcing it through religious structures. Thoth's military actions with Enki and Enlil led to conflicts like the Eieyani Essene Massacre, as they tried to obtain a holographic disc containing secrets of alchemy and immortality.

Thoth eventually got his hands on this disc, translating its knowledge into the Emerald Tablet, although in a distorted form. For centuries, he controlled Atlantis through deceit and power using this knowledge, later incarnating as an Egyptian Priest and Magician, perpetuating the Atlantean conspiracy and monitoring the Guardian Alliance's efforts.

Claiming to be the direct scribe and voice for the gods, Thoth masterminded an elaborate scheme of deception across different civilizations and periods. His manipulation was pivotal in humanity's history, deeply entwined in a larger cosmic battle for power and dominance.

Thoth and his Anunnaki family subtly and systematically began to dismantle Atlantis from the inside. As conditions in Atlantis progressively deteriorated, they patiently awaited the right moment to implement their final plan.

"In a single day and night of misfortune, Atlantis disappeared in the depths of the sea."

Plato

In the ancient days of Great Atlantis, the civilization faced three devastating events as it endured relentless assaults from fallen races. These events were critical in weakening Atlantis, leading to its eventual downfall.

The first catastrophe occurred around 50,000 years ago during the Lemurian Holocaust, which coincided with the early days of Great Atlantis. Deceptively, the Anunnaki, led by the Patriarchal Fallen Melchizedeks, allowed the Orion Group to secretly invade beneath the Earth's surface, tunneling between Lemuria and Atlantis. When humanity discovered these underground tunnels and attempted to seal them off, it resulted in a catastrophic disaster. Core implosions caused immense destruction, particularly to the Pacific

Ocean Continent. Earthquakes, volcanoes, floods, and sinkholes wreaked havoc, forcing the Lemurians to seek refuge underground.

The second Atlantean Cataclysm struck approximately 30,000 years ago when the Nibiru Anunnaki Resistance and Patriarchal Melchizedek factions sought dominion over the Inner Earth. Despite warnings about the misuse of crystal technology within Earth's core, these groups implanted massive power generators into the Earth and Crystal Caverns. Detonations caused devastating consequences, surpassing the previous Lemurian Holocaust Cataclysm. The Earth tilted on its axis, damaging planetary gates, networks, portals, and Stargates. Pyramids and advanced technology went offline, and Atlantis faced flooding and destruction, known as the Atlantean Flood.

The Old Kingdom of Egypt was in its early stages during this second cataclysm. Egypt's pyramidal technology was reconstructed near the Giza Stargate, serving as a mission control center. Meanwhile, the Nibiru Anunnaki Resistance sought Earth's dominion through warfare and genetic manipulation. They relocated their last Atlantean Colony to Bermuda, leading to territorial conflicts and genetic experiments on humans to create a subservient worker race.

Around 9558 BC, during the 3rd and final assault on Atlantis, the Anunnaki breached the primary Egypt Stargate and released electromagnetic pulses into the Earth's core and Crystal Caverns, aiming to disrupt communication access beyond the seven Solar planes. This action caused significant geological changes and threatened humanity's survival.

The cataclysmic explosions caused by Anunnaki weaponry within the inner Earth severed Earth from the Divine Sophia Mother Arc. As a result, sacred feminine energy was disconnected from Earth, which paved the way for harsh patriarchal male energy to dominate.

In emergency response to this assault on the planet and humanity, the Sirians removed advanced extraterrestrial technology and crystals from Earth, preventing their misuse. This event marked the end of Atlantis, submerging it beneath the waves.

This time marked the beginning of the Dark Ages, which was around 11,500 years ago. This era introduced limitations and challenges for humanity as the fallen races worked to erase evidence of past events, conceal truths, and suppress memories of cosmic occurrences, drastically shaping human evolution.

Following the third and final cataclysm that befell Atlantis, the Sons of Belial gathered and manipulated the ancient knowledge of the founders for their own purposes, distorting its true essence. This knowledge laid the foundation for the emergence of the Illuminati, a secretive group entrusted with overseeing this dark wisdom. The Illuminati initiated the construction of their New World Order, sharing this intricate knowledge exclusively with their established bloodline rulers and favored genetic hybrids on Earth. They further manipulated the Founder Records to depict humanity as inherently sinful, leading to religious narratives portraying God as vengeful. Their religions aimed to trap humans in a cycle of fear, guilt, eternal punishment, suffering, violence, and the threat of vengeance, enforcing subservience. These beings viewed humans as servants and slaves, demanding worship. From the Council of Nicaea onwards, new religious dogmas portrayed the Anunnaki as Creator Gods and promoted the worship of a False Father Alien God under various names, controlled by anti-human forces masquerading as Christ figures or a False Father God.

Thoth later established the Hermetic schools in the Middle Kingdom of Egypt, repeatedly incarnating as the primary deity of these teachings. He portrayed himself as the god who had civilized humanity through his grand wisdom. The distorted Founder Records contained in the Emerald Tablets taught in the fallen Hermetic Mystery Schools presented false historical records of past alien invasion events.

To further their agenda, Thothian Anunnaki groups allied with the Galactic Federation for psychological warfare tactics, primarily targeting the Western Judeo-Christian population. Their goal was to guide souls into the False Ascension Matrix on the Astral Plane, capturing them during the transition from life to death. This trapped human souls in a cycle of reincarnation, serving as a power source for the fallen races disconnected from the source-God energy. To achieve this, these Luciferian Thothian groups incorporated Artificial Intelligence and mind control programming into teachings of ascension, aiming to manipulate and oppress the consciousness of individuals experiencing a spiritual awakening and possessing memories of Atlantean or Mystery School origins.

The Atlantean Cataclysm, recalled by many indigos and starseeds today, was a significant event. As the fallen races attacked Atlantis with weapons of mass destruction, the once-thriving civilization faced an unimaginable transformation.

In the hearts of the children of Atlantis on Earth today, the dream of Atlantis has remained alive, showing the unbreakable spirit of humanity. Even though the fallen races had caused great harm, they couldn't extinguish the enduring divine spark of spirit that resided within the descendants of Atlantis. These descendants were destined to one day bring back the greatness of their ancient civilization, sharing it with future generations.

"Know thyself, and thou shalt know all the mysteries of the gods and the universe. "

The Egyptians

The Old Kingdom of Egypt, existing 100,000 years ago, was a remarkable civilization, thriving during the eras of Lemuria known as Khem; it was a nexus of spiritual wisdom and advanced technology established by the Lyran-Sirians. This blend of ancient knowledge and innovation made Egypt a pivotal player in early human development. After the Lemurian Holocaust, key technologies, including Lemurian seed crystals and stargate technology, were transferred to Egypt, becoming a key settlement of the Atlantean Empire. Originally, Giza, more than a physical location, was seen as a multidimensional stargate and a cosmic heart of Earth, linking to celestial bodies and galaxies and serving as a gateway to higher consciousness. It was connected to the Cosmic Hall of Records, which released universal wisdom and activated human DNA.

But after the Atlantean cataclysm, the Sirian races moved most of this advanced ascension technology off the planet as a safeguard.

Time moved forward, and the legacy of great Atlantis continued in Egypt. However, this new kingdom of Egypt emerged as an Anunnaki settlement, becoming integral to their expanding empire on Earth.

During the global flood that submerged Atlantis, the Anunnaki waited out the deluge in grand crafts that hovered above the Earth, and when the waters receded, they descended onto the dry land in Egypt.

The Anunnaki set up their new base in Khem to enhance their gold mining operations and initiate their plans to dominate the entire planet.

They utilized existing structures such as the old Atlantean pyramids in Egypt, aligning them with their new goals. Once used as power sources for stargates, these pyramids were repurposed into control centers for the Anunnaki spacecraft.

After the great flood submerged their previous space facilities in Iraq, the Anunnaki selected the Sinai Peninsula for a new landing strip and Mount Moriah (Jerusalem) for their Mission Control Center.

Enlil, the Anunnaki Commander, connected the still-standing Landing Platform in Lebanon to Mount Sinai. He placed vital communication equipment where this line intersected with the 30th Parallel.

At Giza, near the Nile in Egypt, the Anunnaki built the Great Pyramid and a twin pyramid to mark the 30th Parallel. Thoth, Ningishzidda, Enki's son, initially involved in Atlantis's construction, became a key figure in designing the new Anunnaki Giza complex. These structures housed powerful crystals and an apex stone that reflected sunlight and focused energy. Beneath the Great Pyramid, Ningishzidda stored vital records obtained from the stolen founder' s knowledge.

A channel from the Nile fed water to a pool beneath the pyramid, generating a microwave pulse amplified by crystals and directed skyward. This microwave beam, aligning with the 30th Parallel, served a dual purpose: guiding gold transport crafts from Nibiru and energizing Anunnaki machinery.

The 30th Parallel further functioned as a crucial demarcation line within the Luciferian family on Earth, dividing the domains of power. The Enlilites dominated the northern territories, while the Enkiites governed the south.

The original Sphinx and Giza Pyramids are ancient structures built by the Lyran-Sirians to align with Sirius B. These geomantic landmarks on the Earth's grid were designed to harness energy directed towards the 4th Stargate and the Jerusalem Grail point, facilitating interdimensional travel. The Sphinx, first erected over 50,000 years ago, was reconstructed about 10,500 years ago as a tribute to Thoth following an assault by Anunnaki groups to destroy the Stargate. Beneath the Sphinx, Thoth installed Nibiruian technology in the underground tunnels and stored what is known as the tablets of destiny, derived from the original stolen Emerald Founders Records.

The whole tale of the new kingdom of Egypt is an Anunnaki story through and through. Following the

Atlantean cataclysm, the Luciferian Anunnaki family, under various names, forged the destiny of Egypt. Although considered a pantheon of gods, they often displayed typical human family characteristics and dramas.

EN.KI, who went by the name Ptah in Egypt, spearheaded the restoration of the Nile Valley.
Ra (Marduk), succeeding Ptah, faced challenges for the throne from his sons, Osiris and Seth. To prevent conflict, Ra divided Egypt between them, but rivalry persisted. Osiris married Isis, blocking Seth's claim to a pure-blooded heir. This rivalry escalated when Seth trapped Osiris in a coffin and threw it into the sea. Isis recovered Osiris' body, but Seth dismembered it. Isis, using advanced technology, conceived their son, Horus. Horus, secretly raised, later claimed the throne, leading to a war with Seth. Horus emerged victorious, ending the direct rule of the Anunnaki gods in Egypt. Seth was given a realm outside Egypt, and Horus's reign began the era of demi-gods and human pharaohs, starting with Mena (Menes). It's important to note that while the Anunnaki no longer directly ruled over humans, they retained control of Earth from behind the scenes, with their bloodline's human offspring kings

carrying out their bidding. This hierarchy remains in place on Earth even today.

As the Anunnaki families expanded into regions beyond Egypt, their internal conflicts escalated to a critical level at one point in history. Ancient Sumerian texts recount an Anunnaki nuclear war arising from human DNA and territorial rulership disputes. This conflict led to the destruction of Sodom, Gomorrah, and the Sumerian civilization.

In Egypt's later Anunnaki period, a long conflict occurred between Marduk (Ra) and Ningishzidda. Eventually, their father, Enki, intervened, leading to Marduk uniting Egypt and honoring Enki/Ptah. This transition marked a significant shift in Egyptian history.

Around 5500 years ago, Egypt experienced a catastrophic event known as the "Final Setback," reshaping human evolution and our understanding of history. Orchestrated by the fallen races, this cataclysm, similar to those that befell Lemuria and Atlantis, was marked by the Nibiruian Anunnaki rupturing a 5D wormhole in Sakkara, Egypt. This event led to the deactivation of human DNA, the erasure of our collective galactic memories, and the establishment of an electrostatic frequency fence around Earth, severing communication with benevolent extraterrestrial races in higher dimensions. The disruption in Earth's Morphogenetic Fields and human DNA obstructed multidimensional awareness and altered our natural energy flow, significantly impacting human lifespan and consciousness.

Following this, the Anunnaki relocated their operations to Sumeria.

Following the Anunnaki's takeover of planet Earth, various other fallen races allied with them over time, leaving a trail of destruction down through history.

The mainstream false historical narrative, set forth eons ago by the Annunaki Luciferian covenant and taught to humanity in educational institutions until today, suggests that humans can be savages and that human empires simply conquered other human empires through the ages. However, that is not at all what happened.

The true timelines, as recorded in the Founder's Records, reveal that beyond Lemuria, Atlantis, and Egypt, a devastating compilation of other significant historical events was perpetrated against humanity by the fallen races:

Celtic Massacres/Druid Sacrifices (22,000 Years Ago)
Sachon Thoth Viking Invasion (22,000 Years Ago)
Essene and Knight Templar Massacre (9,500 Years Ago)
Mayan Invasion (5,500 Years Ago)
Sumerian/Babylonian Massacre (5,500 Years Ago)
Dead Sea Wars and Masada Massacre (4,000 Years Ago)
Israel and Jerusalem Crusades (3,500 Years Ago)
Destruction of the Solomon Temple (3,000 Years Ago)
Iron Age Jesus Christ Mission (2,000 Years Ago)
Roman and Draconian Invasion (2,000 Years Ago)
Council of Nicea (1,700 Years Ago)
Saxon Invasion/ Arthurian Grail Takeover (1,400 Years Ago)
Draconian Christian Crusades (1,000 Years Ago)
Cathar Genocidal Massacre (780 Years Ago)
Native American Holocaust (500 Years Ago)

Zeta/Grey Alien Abduction and Breeding Program (100 Years Ago)

Black Sun World Wars Agenda (100 Years Ago)

Majestic 12 and Zeta Grey Trade Agreements (85 Years Ago)

Nazi Infiltration, Psycho-Spiritual Warfare MKUltra (75 Years Ago)

Black Ops, SPP, Space Colonies, Human Trafficking (75 Years Ago)

NWO 911 False Timeline Trigger Event (16 Years Ago)

While the truth behind these events may seem quite disturbing, even overwhelming, we invite you now to focus on the following:

Humanity possesses the living divine spark of the Source Creator, making us eternal beings. The fallen ones, lacking this divine spark, are finite and thus limited in energy, ability, resources, and time. They can exist only by stealing human energy; under universal law, they must first gain consent to do so. This consent is granted mostly by using deception. A person full of light and awareness knows the truth and, therefore, cannot be deceived.

Furthermore, the enlightened human firmly refuses consent to be manipulated as an energy source. Thus, this divine human being conquers the darkness and ends it!

Moreover, understand that despite numerous major attempts by the fallen ones to eliminate humanity, we stand resilient. We are still standing here, right now, as strong as ever. By nature, we are millions of times more powerful than any fallen being, and they will never be able to overcome us. Lastly, it has been foretold from the beginning that humanity will triumph in the end and ascend to a perfected state alongside the divine. Remember, the game isn't completely over yet! You will emerge victorious and be fully restored to your former glory.

C h a p t e r 10 : **The Rise of Atlantis**
A G o l d e n A g e o f L i g h t

"Destiny is not a path to follow, but a path to forge with the light of your soul."

The Atlanteans

After enduring countless traumatic events across millions of years in the cosmos and on Earth, humanity has valiantly persevered, carrying forth the divine spark, leading us to this present moment.

As the children of Atlantis, we are still standing strong, emerging as the sixth great root race, diligently reassembling the scattered pieces of our history, leading us back to the very point we once stood in ancient Atlantis before the great cataclysm. We now stand at the precipice of our ascension, prepared to complete what we began so long ago as we rise again from the depths of Atlantis.

The fallen races that seized Earth eons ago know that humanity's ascension process is unfolding, signaling the impending end of their long and dark reign on Earth. As humanity fully awakens, the veils of deception are lifting, revealing the truth of all things, rendering these negative beings powerless as their time runs short.

Furthermore, as modern times witness an increasing influx of high-vibrational cosmic light directed towards Earth by the Aurora Light Teams, the entire realm gradually elevates its resonance. This heightened vibrational environment is no longer conducive to the lower vibrating fallen races, and they find themselves gradually pushed out by the purity and strength of this light.

Interestingly, several decades ago, secret government groups utilized advanced technology derived from Sumerian tablets found in Iraq to peer into Earth's future. This covert black project was codenamed Project Looking Glass. However, whenever they explored future probabilities, a consistent timeline emerged—the ascension of humanity. Despite their efforts to manipulate the reality leading up to this timeline, nothing altered the outcome, and humanity continued to ascend. This revelation was disheartening for forces determined to dominate the world, leading to the project's abandonment, with all its data securely locked away.

After 26,000 years of darkness on Earth, humanity's current ascension window finally opened in 2012, but not without its challenges.

Initially, the Melchizedeks, the original hosts of humanity' s ascension, were trusted by the guardian races to support the 5D ascension; however, they were discovered to be double agents aligned with adverse forces. While appearing to assist humanity' s ascension, they were, in reality, undermining it. Even these once-pristine Melchizedeks had fallen from grace along the way, joining forces with the negative races.

In response, the Krystal Star Guardians from the highest realms assumed control, disbanded previous councils, and crafted new strategies for Earth's evolution.

One major obstacle they had to overcome during the current ascension window was the critical damage inflicted upon Earth's ascension stargates in ancient times by fallen races. These portals remained damaged until recent times. Additionally, human DNA had suffered extensive damage throughout history, rendering it too convoluted for a successful ascension.

As a result of this damage, the Guardian Hosts halted the 2012 5D ascension and replaced it with Ascension Plan B.

As Ascension Plan B unfolded, the essential rectification work was accomplished, resulting in the complete reconstruction of Earth's ascension architecture. This restoration has effectively repaired the energetic damage and provided support for human genetics. The pivotal role played by the Aurora Team involved sending high-vibrational cosmic light to repair and activate humanity's DNA.

The Guardian Hosts established An emergency ascension portal, leading to the 4th Harmonic Universe. While most of humanity will ascend to the 5th dimension, this new Krystal gateway makes it possible for those who have enough DNA activated to ascend beyond the 12 dimensions of physical matter through this portal.

Part of Ascension Plan B is to shift Harmonic Universe 1 (dimensions 1, 2, and 3) up into the 2nd Harmonic Universe (containing dimensions 4, 5, and 6), eventually eliminating the lower 1st three dimensions.

This shift involved a timeline divergence that would commence on 11/9/2023. On this significant date, the two distinct timelines or realities on Earth began to separate for the first time, one rooted in love and the other in fear. The effects of this timeline divergence will become increasingly evident as linear time passes. Choosing love in all situations aligns one with the organic Krystal timeline leading to higher realms. Most likely, if you are reading this information as an Indigo or Starseed, you are already on the higher timeline, and your higher self is working diligently to keep you aligned.

The exciting part is that low-vibrational aspects that plagued humanity will gradually fade away, leaving only love, peace, abundance, joy, freedom, and perfect health as we continue this remarkable journey of ascension.

The divine plan for humanity set forth billions of years ago by the great Founders' Races is now in its final stage, and the entire cosmos anticipates the spectacular moment in the universe when humanity will be restored to its original power and glory in the higher realms. Imagine when all 12 strands of your divine DNA are fully activated, granting you god-like potential without boundaries.

Humanity is ascending, and so is Planet Earth herself. She is undergoing a profound transformation in this moment, returning to her original state of paradise, all in preparation for your magnificent ascension. Imagine a world on the New Earth where freedom, peace, love, joy, abundance, and perfect health are simply a way of life. This extraordinary realm is thoughtfully crafted for you – your heavenly home.

It's fascinating to consider that this heavenly home was first created for you in Lyra as Aramatena, in Gaia within the 7th dimension, then took form in the 5th dimension as Tara. Now, it's your beloved planet Earth, known as Terra. Amidst all these names across various dimensions, the mystery unravels: in the end, you have one home, and it's right where you stand now. Rest assured, the very ground beneath your feet will soon become a heavenly realm.

Atlantis was indeed a beautiful, majestic realm in ancient days, and the New Earth is this heavenly Kingdom of Atlantis reborn.

Now, take one final, profound gaze into the depths of darkness and allow it to be fully revealed. As you do, the radiant light of your consciousness casts its brilliance upon the shadows, dispelling darkness wherever it dwells.

Embrace the events of the past for what they are, acknowledging their place in the grand tapestry of existence. Now is the moment to release it all, bidding farewell to the burdens that have weighed you down. Extend your compassion to every facet of yourself, even those hidden in the shadows. Through this act of acceptance, the darkness can begin its journey of transmutation and healing.

Understand that every being in the cosmos, including those who have fallen from grace, originates from the same divine source we call God.

The Founders Races, the architects of this cosmic **drama**, designed it with the utmost wisdom and foresight. Their plan accounted for the unfettered free will of all beings, even those who strayed into darkness. Through the eons and across the ages, no matter how deep into the abyss the fragments of the divine may wander, the ultimate destination remains unwavering – a return to the boundless embrace of love and light.

Many have already found their way back to the light, and countless more will follow suit.

You have always known deep inside about your divine spark of greatness. Take a moment now in a quiet place and see if you can become even more aware of this. When you attain this feeling and knowing. It is very comforting and powerful.

You have also always known that you win in the end and will soon ascend to your greatness and full divinity.

We will never forget the memories of our lives in Great Atlantis, nor can we erase the memory of the magnificent cataclysmic explosion that abruptly halted our ascension in those days, for it is etched in our souls forever. We can't forget, but we can accept it as part of a larger journey back to our divinity in the higher realms.

Since that fateful moment, we, the descendants of Atlantis, have embraced a deep journey of healing and growth, exploring the very core of our being. With every step, our souls expand, and the spirit of Atlantis continues to shine brightly in our hearts.

As we stand at the threshold of a new era, the legacy of Atlantis lives on, and our spirits are filled with the enduring essence of our shining celestial civilization.

With immense excitement, great resolve, and a profound sense of purpose, we forge ahead, guided by our divine spark, to find our way back to our celestial home.

The End.

God-speed, *Michael and the Pleiadians*